Ancient
Egypt

Archaeology Unlocks the Secrets of Egypt's Past

NATIONAL GEOGRAPHIC INVESTIGATES

Ancient Egypt

Archaeology Unlocks the Secrets of Egypt's Past

By Jill Rubalcaba

Janice Kamrin, Consultant

NATIONAL GEOGRAPHIC

Washington, DC

4

Contents

◁ This painting from the tomb of Nefertari shows the goddess Isis leading the queen by
the hand. Nefertari was the wife of Ramses II, who ruled in the 13th century B.C.

< The Great Sphinx at Giza is one of the most instantly recognizable monuments of
the ancient world. It was built around 2500 B.C.

Pyramids! Mummies! The mysterious Sphinx! Hieroglyphs! If you are reading this book, I'm guessing that you are fascinated by these traces of the ancient past and want to know more about them. I feel the same way. I am an Egyptologist, and I spend most of my time learning about ancient Egypt and sharing what I find out with other people. I'm very lucky, because I live in Egypt, and I work with Zahi Hawass, the most famous Egyptologist in the world.

I think that you will find this book a wonderful introduction to ancient Egypt. You'll learn things about pyramids and mummies and hieroglyphs, and also about the people who lived in ancient Egypt thousands of years ago. I hope that you enjoy this book, and that it encourages you to go and find out more!

Janice Kamrin
Cairo, 2006

> Egyptologist Janice Kamrin examines the hieroglyphs on an obelisk of red granite in the garden of the Egyptian Museum.

Map of Important Egyptian Archaeological Sites

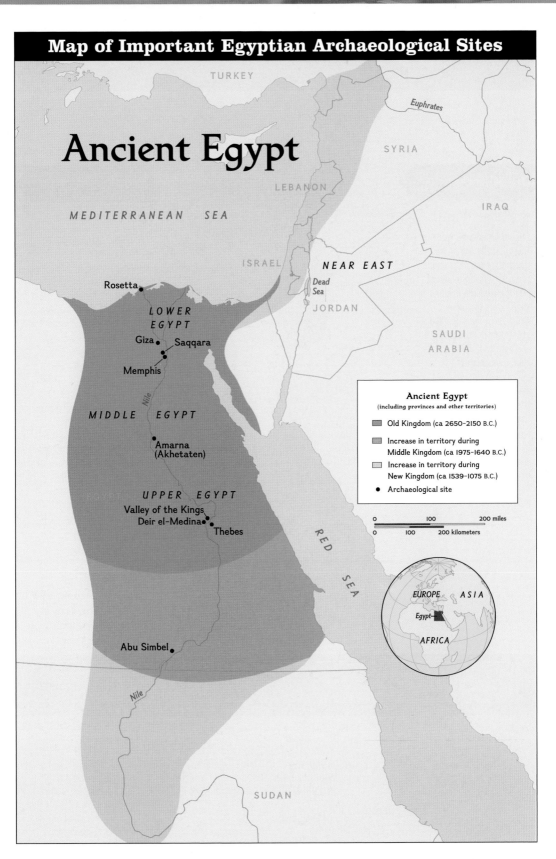

Ancient Egypt

TURKEY

Euphrates

SYRIA

LEBANON

MEDITERRANEAN SEA

IRAQ

ISRAEL

NEAR EAST

Dead Sea

Rosetta

JORDAN

LOWER EGYPT

SAUDI ARABIA

Giza • Saqqara

Memphis

Nile

MIDDLE EGYPT

Amarna (Akhetaten)

UPPER EGYPT

Valley of the Kings
Deir el-Medina • Thebes

RED SEA

Ancient Egypt
(including provinces and other territories)

Old Kingdom (ca 2650-2150 B.C.)

Increase in territory during Middle Kingdom (ca 1975-1640 B.C.)

Increase in territory during New Kingdom (ca 1539-1075 B.C.)

• Archaeological site

0   100   200 miles
0   100   200 kilometers

EUROPE   ASIA

Egypt

AFRICA

Abu Simbel

Nile

SUDAN

THREE MAJOR PERIODS OF
Egyptian History

Old Kingdom

ca 2650—2150 B.C.

The Old Kingdom is best known as the age of the pyramids, the most famous of which are those built at Giza for the kings Khufu, Khafre, and Menkaure. When these kings reigned at Memphis in the 26th and 25th centuries B.C. power was highly centralized, though royal authority lessened in the later part of the period. Towards the end of the Old Kingdom, a succession of poor harvests caused widespread famine and poverty. The country then fragmented and the First Intermediate Period began.

Middle Kingdom

ca 1975—1640 B.C.

After the First Intermediate Period, when Egypt dissolved into a number of separate states, the country was reunified under Mentuhotep I. Mentuhotep ruled from Thebes but his successors moved the capital to a site near Memphis, where it had been located during the Old Kingdom. Senwosret I conducted several successful campaigns against the Nubians, who lived to the south. Towards the end of the period, Egypt once again began to fragment. The north fell to foreign invaders, the Hyksos.

< A statue of the god Anubis, who guided the dead in the underworld

Timeline of Egyptian History

3000 B.C.	2500	2000	
ca 3050 Foundation of Egyptian state with Memphis as its capital	ca 2550 Work begins on Great Pyramid at Giza	ca 2150 Egypt fragments into smaller states	ca 1900 Senwosret I conquers Nubia	ca 1630 Egypt to fore invad the Hy
ca 3150 First use of writing	ca 2650 Step pyramid built for pharaoh Djoser		ca 1975 Egypt reunified under Mentuhotep I	

First Intermediate Period

Se Interme P

Old Kingdom   Middle Kingdom

New Kingdom

ca 1539—1075 B.C.

The pharaoh Ahmose drove the Hyksos out of Egypt and reunited the country. The rulers who followed him conquered large parts of Nubia and West Asia. As a result of this policy of military expansion, the army became a force in Egyptian politics. Many rulers were buried in the Valley of the Kings, which was situated near Thebes. One of the most famous of the New Kingdom pharaohs was Akhenaten, who tried to establish a new religion.

> This gold collar is made in the shape of the vulture goddess Nekhbet.

ca 1353 Beginning of reign of Akhenaten

1000

500

O A.D.

ca 1075 Egypt dissolves into a number of separate kingdoms

671 Egypt invaded by Assyrians

332 Beginning of Greek rule

+90 Thutmose I quers much of t Asia; greatest ent of empire

ca 1332 Beginning of reign of Tutankhamun

ca 1260 Temple of Abu Simbel built in reign of Ramses II

Ahmose drives out of Egypt

ca 1275 Ramses II fights Hittites at Battle of Qadesh

Third Intermediate Period

New Kingdom

Late Period

Greek Rule

Yesterday Comes Alive

CHAPTER 1

How do we learn what we know about the past?

In 1799 a group of French soldiers rebuilding an old fort on the Egyptian coast uncovered a gray slab of granite in the dusty rubble. The stone's surface was covered in strange markings that the soldiers could not read. It would take over 20 years of hard work before anybody could read the markings. The Rosetta Stone, as it became known, would prove to be one of the most important archaeological finds ever made. A fragment of a larger stone, it was the key that unlocked many of the secrets of one of the most long-lived of ancient civilizations: that of Egypt.

< A tourist examines the hieroglyphs on a pharaoh's coffin. Before the Rosetta Stone was deciphered, archaeologists could not understand the ancient writing.

The discovery happened purely by chance. The French general Napoleon Bonaparte had invaded Egypt as part of France's war against Great Britain. He wanted to get control of an important British trade route by setting up defenses along the coast.

That was how Lieutenant Pierre Bouchard found himself leading a corps of engineers to the old fortress north of the town of Rosetta. The fort was small and in bad shape. The soldiers would almost need to knock it down and rebuild it before they could move in.

The soldiers set to work. But working in Egypt was nothing like working in France. The blinding sunlight and breezes peppered with sand caused all kinds of eye problems. Many soldiers lost their eyesight.

∧ This 19th-century painting shows the French general Napoleon Bonaparte leading an expedition across the Egyptian desert.

The relentless Egyptian heat forced soldiers to gulp gallons of water—water they shouldn't have drunk. Many soon buckled over with diarrhea. Others fell from sunstroke. Still, Bouchard pushed them on.

The men knocked down one of the fort's crumbling walls. Then they started to clear the huge pile of rock and sand. The rubble was all the same tan color—except for a gray slab of granite about 4 feet (1.2 m) long. One young soldier wiped away the dust from the stone and noticed carvings in that strange picture writing belonging to the ancient Egyptians. He decided he'd better report the find to his commanding officer.

Sacred carvings

The ancient Egyptians used a system of writing made up of pictures. They called their writing *medu netjer*, which means "words of god." Thousands of years later the Greeks named these picture words *hieroglyphs*, which means "sacred carvings." The Greeks believed the words must be sacred because they found them in tombs and temples. They were everywhere: On the walls, across the ceilings—even the coffins were covered with carvings.

Very few people in ancient Egypt could read or write the

∧ **Writing hieroglyphs was difficult work. The Egyptians used hieratic, and then the demotic script shown here, for everyday writing.**

> **This statue of a seated scribe was made in around 2500 B.C. Scribes were important people.**

complicated script. Being able to write was a profession all by itself. Those who could were called scribes. It took years to learn the skill. While other children were outside playing hockey with sticks made from palm branches and pucks made from leather pouches stuffed with papyrus, the students studying to be scribes practiced writing.

Over time, the hard-to-learn hieroglyphs were replaced by an easier system of writing. Scribes still used the "words of god" in sacred places—on temples and tombs—but for record keeping they adopted a

Code Breaking

Until Jean-François Champollion made his amazing breakthrough in 1822, most experts believed that the system of hieroglyphs used by the ancient Egyptians was symbolic. This means that each picture simply symbolized an object or an idea. A picture of a lion might represent "courage" or it might simply mean "lion." After years of studying Egyptian texts, especially the Rosetta Stone, Champollion focused on the names of famous rulers of ancient Egypt written in hieroglyphs. He figured out that the pictures could represent sounds as well as symbols. Champollion's breakthrough was crucial in helping historians uncover many of ancient Egypt's secrets.

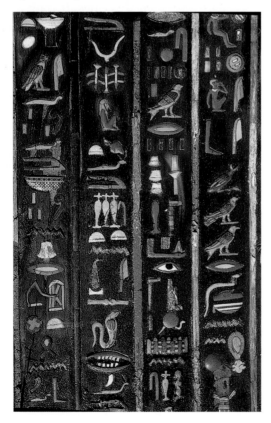

V **These hieroglyphs from the outside of a coffin represent a spell from the Book of the Dead.**

more practical script. They called it *sesh*, which means "writing for documents." Later, the Greeks named this writing demotic. As the centuries passed, fewer and fewer scribes learned the ancient sacred symbols. When the Greeks ruled Egypt (from 332 B.C. to 30 B.C.) their alphabet found its way into Egyptian writing. By the fourth century A.D., no one could read those words drawn in pictures. The hieroglyphs that had been used for more than 3,500 years became a mystery—one that haunted scholars. The words of the ancients were everywhere. But no one knew how to read them.

Secrets of the stone

The three-quarter-ton granite slab Napoleon's soldiers found had been carved in three scripts. Two of the scripts were Egyptian—hieroglyphic and demotic. One was Greek. It appeared as if someone, 2,000 years before, had carved the same message three ways. Napoleon's scholars made copies of what they were now calling the Rosetta Stone. They spread ink over the stone, laid sheets of paper on top of the ink, and then used rollers to transfer the markings onto paper. These copies were sent to scholars all over Europe. Would this four-by-two-and-a-half-foot stone be the clue that cracked the code?

Despite his string of forts along the coastline, Napoleon lost control of Egypt to the British only three years pharaoh, Ptolemy V. The priests thank Ptolemy for the many good things that he has done for the people of Egypt.

With the Greek just beneath the two Egyptian scripts, many scholars believed it wouldn't be long before the hieroglyphic and the demotic were decoded. They were very wrong.

∨ Jean-François Champollion was the man who finally deciphered Egyptian hieroglyphs.

∧ The three sections of the Rosetta Stone were a huge puzzle for linguists trying to match the Greek words to the Egyptian writings.

after he arrived. The British took many of the artifacts that the French had found, including the Rosetta Stone, which was sent back to England under military escort. Plaster casts of the inscriptions were made for universities throughout Europe. The original stone went to the British Museum.

The bottom section in Greek was easily translated. It had been written by a group of priests in 196 B.C. to celebrate the reign of their 13-year-old

∧ After the British victory in Egypt, they shipped many monuments to London, including Cleopatra's Needle.

It would take more than 20 years before the ancient scripts gave up their secrets. An Englishman named Thomas Young made the first real breakthrough. Young had a natural gift for languages. At seven he was fluent in three languages; by the time he turned 14, he had mastered a dozen. Young was sure he would be the first to crack the code. He noticed that a small oval containing certain symbols was repeated throughout the text. Young realized the symbol must represent a name—likely that of the 13-year-old pharaoh Ptolemy V.

Young worked on the demotic lines and figured out many of the words, but the hieroglyphs stumped him. It would take another young genius, Jean-François Champollion, to solve the riddle.

Long after most scholars had thrown up their hands in despair, Champollion doggedly worked at the script, symbol by symbol, from the time he first received a copy when he was 18 in

Quote from the Rosetta Stone

"They shall write the decree on a stela of hard stone in the script of the words of god *[hieroglyphs]*, the script of the documents *[demotic]* and the script of the Ionians *[Greek]* and set it up in the…temples…in the vicinity of the divine image of the pharaoh living forever."

1808, until the time of his death 24 years later. Eventually, after much study, he began publishing details of the meanings of individual hieroglyphs. He had cracked the code.

Unsolved mysteries

The puzzle of the hieroglyphs is just one of the many mysteries of ancient Egypt that have stumped historians. Another is the cause of the death of the boy king Tutankhamun. Was he murdered? In chapter 2 you can learn how archaeologists are using modern medical technology to try to solve the riddle.

Like everyone, archaeologists want to know about the kings who were buried in Egypt's great pyramids. But,

as chapters 3 and 4 show, they are just as interested in the lives of the people who built such monuments, and the bakers who made bread for them. What kind of lives did they lead?

In over 200 years since the Rosetta Stone was discovered, hieroglyphics have taught us much about how the Egyptians lived—and about the place of the dead in Egyptian life. But the process of discovery still goes on. In chapter 6, you will visit a new chamber that was discovered in 2006. Inside was a coffin holding a garland of flowers— but no body. No one knows what that might mean… yet.

▽ Archaeologist Audran Labrousse studies some hieroglyphic writing in the tomb of Pepi I, who reigned in the 24th and 23rd centuries B.C.

CHAPTER 2

Letters in Clay

Who wrote the tablets of Amarna?

In the late 19th century, a peasant woman came across a pile of sun-dried clay tablets while poking through the ruins of the ancient buildings in the Egyptian site of Amarna. She had come to collect some of the crumbling mud-bricks to use as fertilizer for her garden. These tablets did not look very valuable, but they would give us a glimpse into the lives of kings who had ruled over 3,000 years earlier.

< An archaeologist brushes sand away from a ceramic mask at Amarna.

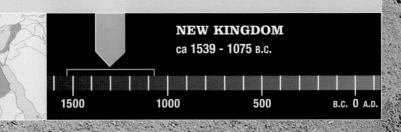

NEW KINGDOM
ca 1539 - 1075 B.C.

1500   1000   500   B.C. 0 A.D.

The peasant woman gathered up all the unbroken tablets and took them to a neighbor, who sold them for a small profit to a local dealer. The dealer sent a few samples to experts in Europe. They found their way into the hands of E. A. Wallis Budge, an Egyptologist who worked at the British Museum. Budge wrote: "When I examined the tablets I found that the matter was not as simple as it looked. In shape and form, and colour and material, the tablets were unlike any I had ever seen in London or Paris, and the writing on all of them was of a most unusual character and puzzled me for hours."

Recognizing that the markings were an ancient type of writing known as cuneiform, Budge made out the words, "to Nimmuriya, king of the land of Egypt." Budge wrote: "The opening words of nearly all the tablets proved them to be letters or dispatches, and I felt certain that the tablets were both genuine and of very great historical importance."

The hunt for tablets

Budge immediately purchased the sample tablets and set out to find more. Word quickly spread about what Budge was up to. The museum curators in all the major European cities ordered their scouts in Egypt to find as many of the tablets as they could and buy them. Today that's illegal. But in the 19th century that's the way it was often done—museums bought looted antiquities on the black market.

We now know that Budge was right. The tablets are letters from the middle years of the 2nd millennium B.C. Nimmuriya was another name for Amenophis III, a pharaoh

◁ This clay tablet is one of almost 400 that make up the Amarna Letters. Many of the letters were addressed to the pharaoh Akhenaten.

∧ **The remains of the palace of Nefertiti at Amarna; Nefertiti was the wife of Akhenaten.**

who ruled Egypt in the 14th century B.C. The letters are from Egypt's neighbors and were written in ancient Babylonian, the diplomatic language of the time. Today scholars call the tablets the Amarna Letters.

Scholars have divided the letters into two groups according to the way that the pharaoh was approached. Those from foreign rulers who thought they were just as important as the pharaoh open by addressing him as "brother." The second group of tablets have a very different tone. Normal people had to grovel when approaching the pharaoh. The author of one letter describes himself as "the dust of your two feet…"

Scholars have deduced that many of the letters were addressed to

Pharaoh Akhenaten, Amenophis III's son. They were often from chiefs who were under attack from Egypt's enemies and needed help. They beg Akhenaten for such things as gold and soldiers. Akhenaten mostly ignored them. He was not a general and a warrior like the pharaohs before him, but a thinker. He had his own ideas for Egypt.

A revolutionary king

After he took the throne in 1353 B.C., Akhenaten began making changes. In the following years he closed the old temples and made the sun-disk god, Aten, the chief god of Egypt. He ordered all mention of the old gods erased from monuments in Thebes. But Thebes and the sun god,

A Magic Spell for Everything

The grandest purchase E. A. Wallis Budge made for the British Museum was a copy of *The Book of the Dead*. It should be named, *The Book for the Dead*, because that's who it was written for—the dead. The book is a collection of magic spells to help the deceased pass safely through the underworld on their way to the afterlife. There were hundreds of different spells in all. Each spell protected the deceased from a different danger. Copies of these spells came in a number of forms. Sometimes they were inscribed on the walls of tombs, but it was more common for them to be written on rolls of papyrus, which were then left in the purchaser's tomb.

< This statue of the pharaoh Akhenaten shows him with a potbelly.

Amun-Re, were closely bound together. So, in the sixth year of his reign, Akhenaten moved the capital. He built a completely new city in middle Egypt. A city he called Akhetaten. The city we call Amarna.

The first Egyptologist to thoroughly excavate Amarna was an Englishman named Flinders Petrie. Petrie was like Akhenaten in at least one way. Akhenaten broke with tradition and changed Egypt; Petrie changed archaeology. Before Petrie archaeologists behaved more like treasure hunters than scholars. They plowed through sites in search of riches and discarded the rest. Petrie's methods were quite different. He recorded every detail. He studied every shovel full of dirt. He mapped every find no matter how small or insignificant it seemed.

Digging through the ruins of the ancient city in the late 19th century, Flinders Petrie was able to identify the building where the Amarna tablets were stored. He also uncovered the remains of the Great Temple of Aten and several royal palaces.

The art Petrie found there was most unusual. Akhenaten had not only changed gods and capitals, but art as well. Traditionally Egyptian artists tried to make their pictures look perfect rather than realistic. This was particularly true of pharaohs, who had been portrayed as young, brave, and strong for thousands of years. Akhenaten, however, instructed his artists to draw what they saw, even when they were portraying him. Artists showed Akhenaten with full breasts and a sagging belly.

∧ This stone block is from one of the temples that Akhenaten built at Karnak. Akhenaten promoted the worship of the sun-disk god Aten.

A unique site

Akhenaten died in 1336 B.C. Soon afterward, the new capital was abandoned. The pharaohs who followed demolished Akhenaten's temples and erased his name. The fact that Akhetaten was only inhabited for a short period means that it is a special site for archaeologists because generations of houses haven't been built on top of one another. This allowed archaeologists to build up a model of what the city would have looked like 3,500 years ago.

Using Computers

The science of archaeology has changed since the days of Budge and Petrie. In fact, it's changing all the time. For example, until recently archaeologists had to glue photographs of fragments of finds to bits of glass so that they could piece them together. Now the whole process can be done on a computer. Archaeologists used both methods when they were trying to reassemble the bricks in the

∧ Photographs of the wall of the Temple of Aten are glued to glass.

walls of the temples that Akhenaten built at Karnak. Computer programs also allow archaeologists to create 3-D images of monuments that can be viewed at any angle. Programs can even recreate ancient lighting conditions.

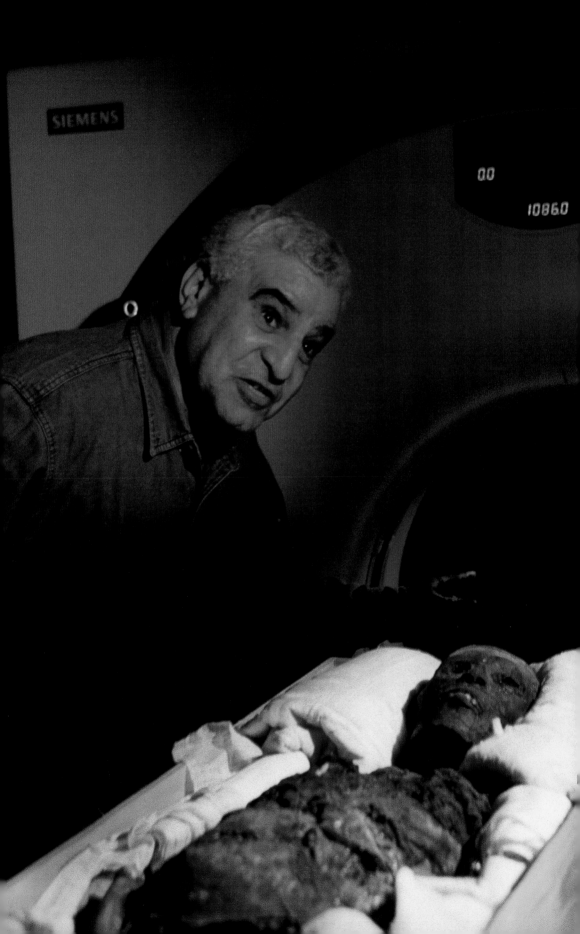

The Tomb of King Tut

CHAPTER 3

How did King Tutankhamun die?

Was he murdered? That was one of the questions Zahi Hawass, the head of Egypt's Supreme Council of Antiquities, hoped to answer with the CT scan he was performing one cloudy Wednesday in January of 2005. It was a cold case. A 3,300-year-old cold case. The victim was the boy king Tutankhamun.

The scientists removed the lid from the gilded coffin. Then they gently carried the wooden box holding King Tutankhamun up the stone steps of

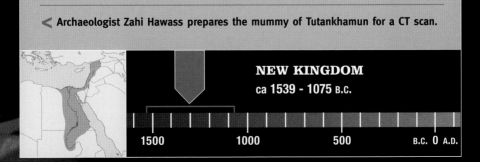

< Archaeologist Zahi Hawass prepares the mummy of Tutankhamun for a CT scan.

NEW KINGDOM
ca 1539 - 1075 B.C.

1500   1000   500   B.C. 0 A.D.

<The gold funerary mask of the boy king Tutankhamun is one of the most recognizable treasures of ancient Egypt.

Tut had not always been treated with such care. When archaeologist Howard Carter found Tutankhamun more than 80 years earlier, archaeologists were only beginning to realize that mummies deserved respect. Then people were more interested in the fantastic treasure that tombs contained.

Royal tombs during Tut's lifetime were located on the west bank of the Nile at Thebes in the Valley of the Kings. Stonemasons carved the tombs out of the cliff walls or into the floor of the valley. Then the kings arranged to have their tombs packed with everything they might need in the afterlife. There were the essentials—food, drink, and clothing. And then there were the ruler's luxuries, such as toys, heirlooms, oils, and perfumes. And finally there were the beautiful masks and jewels that we now associate with the ancient Egyptian pharaohs. It's no wonder thieves came treasure hunting.

the underground tomb to the trailer waiting outside. Inside the trailer scientists peeled back the blanket protecting the mummy before feeding it into the scanner—box and all. Zahi Hawass told the press, "Through the scan, we hope to learn about any diseases Tut had, any kind of injuries, his actual age, and maybe more about how he died."

How Mummies Were Made

When an important person died—one who was wealthy enough to afford to be mummified—his or her body was taken to the Place of Washing to be cleaned up. Next, at the embalmer's workshop, morticians removed the brain with a hook and flushed out the skull with water. The brain was thrown away because no one believed it was important. The morticians removed most of the internal organs, cleaned them, and stored them in jars. It was important to save the whole body for the spirit to inhabit in the next life. Even fingernails and toenails were wrapped with twine to keep them from falling off. Embalmers stuffed and covered the body with a salt called natron to keep it dry.

After 40 days, morticians removed the old stuffing from the body cavity and repacked it with sawdust, rags, and natron. They rubbed the skin with oils to restore its softness. Then the wrapping began. It could take more than two weeks and 500 square yards of linen to properly wrap a body. A whole football field covered in linen would only contain enough cloth to wrap ten bodies. The morticians chanted spells and performed other religious rituals all the way through the process.

Everything was saved—the used sawdust, natron, fluids, and cloth—and stored in large pots. Who knew what bits and pieces might be caught in the debris and needed in the afterlife?

Tomb raiders

Thieves knew where to find the valuables. Most royal graves were looted before the doorway seals had a chance to harden. Once inside the tomb, robbers often headed straight for the mummy. They hacked the mummy apart looking for riches—jewels were often hidden in the bandages. The robbers had so little regard for the dead that they sometimes used the mummified bodies of children as torches to see their way through the tomb.

To thwart thieves pharaohs

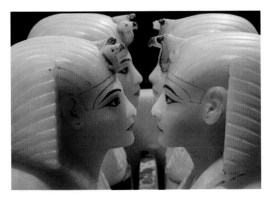

∧ **These four alabaster heads acted as stoppers for the containers that held Tutankhamun's organs.**

kept their tomb locations as secret as possible. They posted guards around the clock, and severely punished tomb robbers, often with impalement on a sharpened stake. Yet despite these efforts, the tombs were broken into and robbed again and again. Finally, to protect what they could of the royal families, the priests officially opened all the tombs, reverently rewrapped the mummies, placed them in plain wooden coffins, and then hid them in empty tombs.

Carter's thrill at finding Tut's tomb quickly turned to dismay

∧ Howard Carter peers at the shrines surrounding Tutankhamun's coffin. The tomb was full of treasures.

when he discovered the doorway seals had been broken—tomb robbers! While Carter and his crew removed the rubble from the stairway they must have wondered if this would be another disappointment. Would this once treasure-packed tomb be empty? What would they find?

Carter peered into a room packed to the ceiling—a jumble of chests piled on top of chairs, chariots, beds, statues, and board games. Sandals, statues, and pottery littered the floor. Everything the king would need in the next life had been crammed into the small space. It would take three years of photographing, cataloging, and clearing the grave goods before Carter finally made his way through to Tut's mummy, concealed inside three coffins.

In a sacred ritual, priests had poured oils over the mummy and the coffin. Unfortunately the oils glued the two together. Tut was stuck. Carter cut the bandages away from Tut's skinny legs and folded arms. But he could not lift the gold mask away from the king's face and shoulders. He was afraid he'd have to use a hammer and chisel, but in the end he was successful prying it off with heated knives. Underneath the mask, Tut's skin was brittle and cracked. His head was shaven. His lips glued shut. And his ears pierced. Although his nostrils had been packed with linen, his nose had flattened under the bandages.

A mysterious ruler

Although he is one of the most famous of all the rulers of Egypt, not much is known about Tutankhamun's life. He was probably only nine years old when he became king. Some historians believe that his father was Akhenaten, the pharaoh who replaced the ancient gods of Egypt with a single sun god, Aten, though Tut may have been the son of the previous

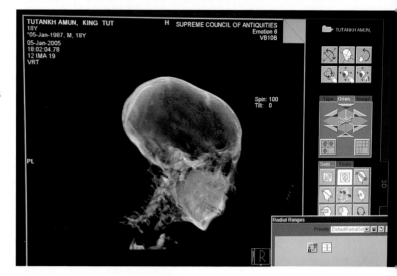

> This CT scan shows the skull and neck of Tutankhamun, over 3,300 years after he died. The scan proved that the pharaoh was not killed by a blow to the head.

∨ A team of conservators work to preserve two wooden boats that were found in the tomb of Tutankhamun.

king, Amenophis III. One of the major changes that Tutankhamun and his advisors carried out during his reign was to reestablish Thebes and Memphis as the two most important cities in Egypt—Akhenaten had tried to create a new capital at Akhetaten, but his changes proved unpopular. Tutankhamun also promoted the old gods, but did not have much time to make his mark on Egypt. He died in the ninth year of his reign—at only 18—and was hastily buried.

Case solved?

The results of the CT scan are in. They give us a few more details about the life of the boy king. They tell us that Tutankhamun was well-fed and healthy, though he had an overbite that ran in the family and an impacted wisdom tooth. He did not suffer from malnutrition or disease in childhood. Most importantly, the results show that the boy king did not die from a blow to the head, as some people have suggested. There are some loose fragments of bone in his skull, but the damage could not have been caused while he was alive. Murder could not be ruled out, however. As Zahi Hawass has pointed out, there are things that the CT scan can't show, such as whether Tut was poisoned. Was he murdered? The jury's still out.

The Tomb Builders

Why do archaeologists care about trash?

Imagine 3,000 years from now archaeologists trying to understand how you lived by studying the remains of your neighborhood. Just to make it more difficult, for centuries people have been poking through every home taking anything of value and selling it on the Internet. Valuables are scattered all over the world. Your first-edition Harry Potter collection? Sold. That grand piano in the house on the corner? Sold. Sold to collectors all over the world. No one bothered to

< An archaeologist examines a tomb in the builders' cemetery at Giza.

NEW KINGDOM
ca 1539 - 1075 B.C.

1500   1000   500   B.C. 0 A.D.

record where these items were found or who bought them. How will these future archaeologists know that you were the one who read Harry Potter and not the one who played Mozart?

Confusing? You bet. That's the challenge for archaeologists excavating Deir el-Medina, an Egyptian village that was home to the workers who built the tombs in the Valley of the Kings. If they want to understand the daily life of the tomb builders who lived in this village 3,000 years ago, they

< This ancient ceramic vessel used for grain storage was found at Deir el-Medina.

must first assemble the pieces. Pieces scattered all over the world. Pieces picked up and sold before careful records were kept by archaeologists. Today if archaeologists discover an artifact they record its exact location on a site map. They can reconstruct a room, a house, or a village and learn a lot about the people who lived there. At Deir el-Medina, long after the treasure seekers had come and gone, many archaeologists dug for season after season in the village. Pooling all their information will take decades.

V The remains of the village of Deir el-Medina. About 3,500 years ago it was home to the workers who built royal tombs nearby.

Some of the most important discoveries at Deir el-Medina were made by the French archaeologist Bernard Bruyère. He worked at the village between 1922 and 1951. Unlike many of the others before him, Bruyère was not particularly interested in the cemetery overlooking the village. Instead Bruyère was interested in the village itself. And what interested him most was the village's trash. If you think about it, your trash reveals a lot—what you had for dinner, what magazines you read, how well you did on last week's vocabulary quiz and what words you were learning. The village's trash told Bruyère a great deal, too. And it was helpful that thieves weren't interested in it, so it hadn't been scattered all over the world.

Lives of the tomb builders

Today we call the tomb builders' village Deir el-Medina, but 3,000 years ago the workmen called it *Pa-demi,* which means simply "the

∧ This statue is of a priest and judge called Kai. Kai and his family were important enough to have three tombs at Giza.

town." The town was built near the Valley of the Kings in a waterless, rocky cup in the hills. The workers' laundry was done for them because they could not easily get to the Nile to wash their clothes. And teams of donkeys brought fresh water daily to the village. Every month workmen were paid in food and clothes.

The tomb builders and their families lived quite comfortably.

In order to get to the Valley of the Kings from the village, the workmen first had to hike along a winding mountain path. During the week, rather than walking all the way home, they camped on a level spot along the pathway in a group of stone huts.

Guardians of the Tomb handed out copper chisels to the stonecutters at the work site. The stonecutters chopped their way hundreds of feet into the soft limestone cliffs, while the draftsmen laid out the tomb's design with grid lines, and painters mixed their pigments. The artists worked by

the light of oil lamps with wicks that had been treated with salt to keep them from smoking. The foremen, Overseers of Construction in the Great Place, made sure everything went smoothly.

Security was important. Police patrolled the west bank, controlling who came and went from the Valley of the Kings. Door-Keepers of the Tomb guarded tomb entrances and the Guardians of the Tomb watched over tools and construction materials.

Building a village close to the Valley of Kings and far from the Nile had its problems. One of the biggest had to be providing water for 100 or more people. Carrying all that water

◁ The building of all of Egypt's great monuments—here the pyramid of Khafre at Giza—required huge numbers of laborers.

for a trash pit. Over the years it gradually filled up with garbage, garbage that would one day be discovered by Bernard Bruyère.

Tales from the past

Among the things Bernard Bruyère found in the pit were chunks of pottery that the villagers had used for scrap paper. Bruyère found everything from shopping lists to ghost stories to love poems. There were magic spells to prevent nightmares: "Come out with what you have seen so that your dumbness ceases and your dreams retreat. May fire come out against the thing that frightened you!" There was even a note from a teacher demanding homework, "Bring your chapter and come!" And the student's frantic promise, "I will do it!"

In a community of skilled artisans, where everyone was free from farm chores, school was possible for many of the village children, not just the sons of scribes. They would have learned to read and write by copying sentences on pieces of pots (later to be thrown away in the trash pit). Children would learn the classics, such as *The Tale of Sinuhe*, the story of a pharaoh's guard named Sinuhe who fled from Egypt when he thought he might be accused of a plot against the king. They would also learn songs, such as *The Hymn to the Nile*, which sings the praises of

must have been difficult, and delays could be deadly.

To solve the problem the villagers tried to dig a well. They dug 170 feet (52m) down, climbing in and out of the pit by way of a staircase that spiraled around the walls of the hole. Eventually, however, the villagers gave up. They used the dry hole a woman called Naunakht. Naunakht wasn't a queen or a particularly important person: the reason that she's still famous today is that archaeologists have discovered her will, which was written on a piece of papyrus. It seems that Naunakht was fairly well off. When she was 12 years old, she married an old man named Kenherkhepeshef, who was the village scribe, an extremely important position in ancient Egypt. He died before the couple could have any children, and Naunakht inherited most of his considerable property. Naunakht remarried, but she must have been fond of her first husband because

∧ This statue depicts a woman grinding wheat.

> This table bearing loaves of bread was found in the tomb of an architect who worked for the pharaoh Amenophis III.

the yearly flood that brings rich black earth to the farmlands.

Naunakht's will

Sometimes a scrap of paper can help us build up a really detailed picture of someone's life. One person who lived at Deir el-Medina whom we know quite a lot about is

Baking Bread the Traditional Way

We know that the main food of the tomb builders was bread, because many important people were buried with loaves of bread for the afterlife. But how did the ancient Egyptians make it? And what did it taste like?

Egyptologists have known the answer to the first question for some time. Pictures of people making bread decorate the walls of many tombs. It was baked in clay pots, which came in two halves. Dough was put into the bottom half, which was placed in hot coals. The other half of the pot was heated to a great temperature and then placed on top. The combined heat was enough to bake the bread.

>Pots are heated in an open fire as part of an attempt to re-create ancient baking techniques.

In order to find out what ancient Egyptian bread tasted like you would have to make it in exactly the same way, with the kind of ingredients that were used in ancient times. In 1991 a team from the University of Chicago did just that. They used a rare kind of wheat called emmer, which no longer grows in Egypt and had to be imported from California. The experiment was a success. The loaf tasted like modern sourdough bread.

she named her eldest child Kenherkhepeshef.

When Naunakht grew old, she became dependent on her children to look after her. It seems that some of them were lazy and neglected their duties. When she turned 78, she disinherited half of them. Naunakht went to court to have her will drawn up and recorded. "I have grown old and they do not look after me in their turn. Whoever has aided me, to them I will give of my property; he who has not aided me, I will not give of my property." Naunakht's children had to swear that they would not contest the will at a later date.

The will is unclear whether three or four of the children were to be disinherited, but one thing seems certain: she had a favorite. It looks as if her oldest son Kenherkhepeshef always stayed in her good favor. The will makes a special point of saying that, on top of the rest of his inheritance, he should receive a bronze washing bowl.

CHAPTER 5

The Pyramid Builders

What was it like to work on the pyramids?

Just south of the Great Pyramid and the Sphinx of Giza, archaeologist Zahi Hawass stands over a grave. He watches a member of his team digging below. The man empties a trowel full of sand into a rubber bucket. When the bucket is full another team member will haul it up and carry it over to more workers waiting with sieves, ready to carefully sift the sand. The sieves have two layers, one coarse like chicken-wire, and the second as fine as mosquito netting.

◁ Restoration work is carried out on the Great Sphinx at Giza. The limestone monument is slowly being eroded by pollution.

OLD KINGDOM
ca 2650 - 2150 B.C.

2500   2000   1500   B.C. 1000

Sifting is hot, dusty work, but the team will miss nothing. Not a bone or a bead.

Hawass points to something poking out of the sand. The man sets his trowel aside and picks up a paint brush. He gently brushes the sand away from darkened bone. A skull, a jaw, a shoulder, then an entire skeleton is uncovered. The body has been buried on its side, its knees tucked to its chest. It faces east toward the rising sun. The top of its head points north, toward the path that the pharaoh's spirit will travel each night from the

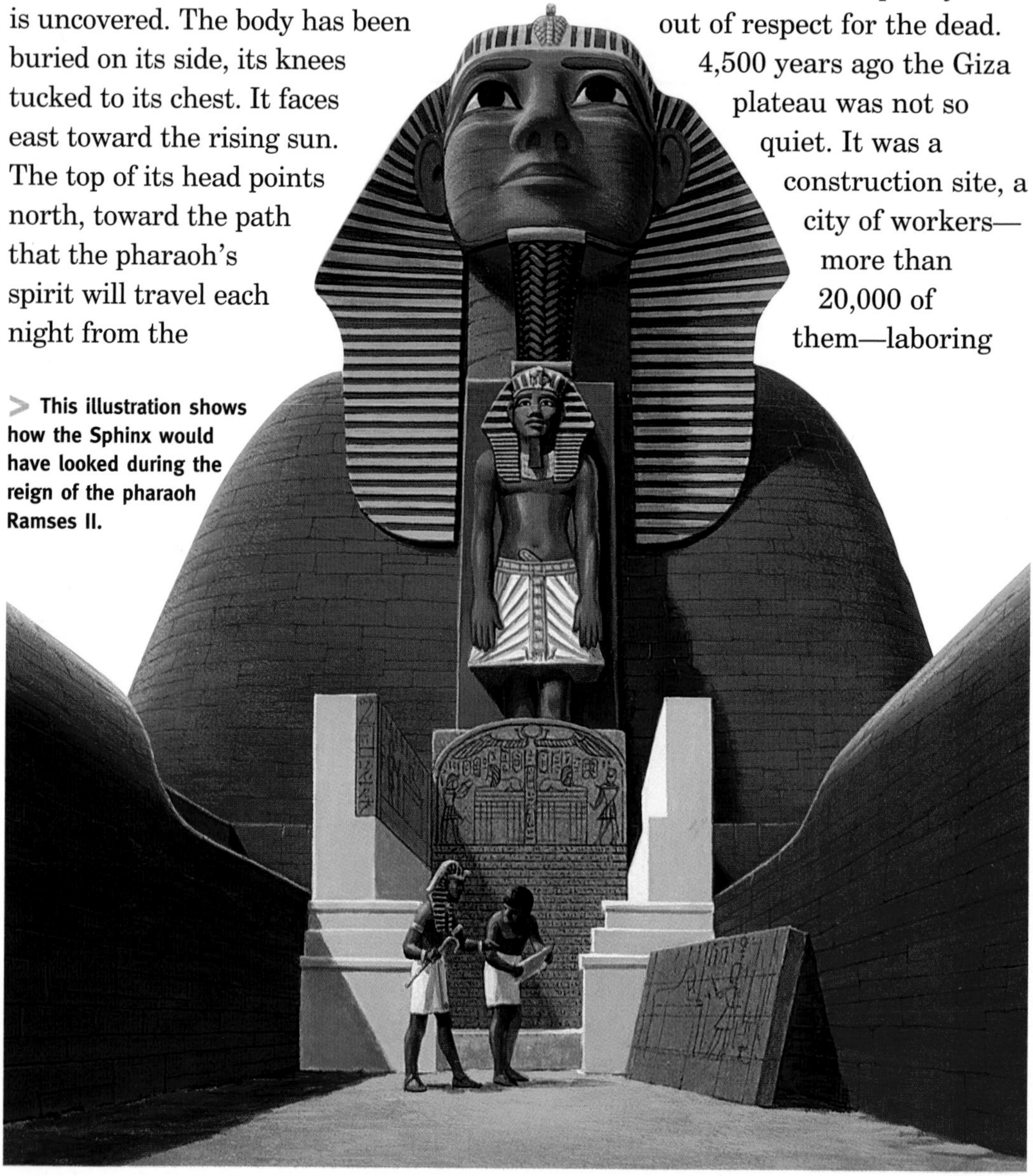

> This illustration shows how the Sphinx would have looked during the reign of the pharaoh Ramses II.

pyramid to the stars. The man working in the grave leaves the skeleton in place for the team's bone specialist. He picks up a small bead and passes it to Hawass. This pyramid builder was a woman.

A city of workers

Hawass's team works quietly out of respect for the dead. 4,500 years ago the Giza plateau was not so quiet. It was a construction site, a city of workers— more than 20,000 of them—laboring

The Pyramid Still Stands

In 130 B.C., the Greek poet Antipator of Sidon made a list of the Seven Wonders of the World. Six of the seven have vanished, but 4,500 years after its creation, the Great Pyramid still stands. Its brilliant white limestone casing has long ago been stripped. Some of its stone blocks have been taken for building projects elsewhere. And yet, this wonder remains a symbol of grandeur and permanence.

∧ Khufu's pyramid is the oldest of the Seven Wonders of the World.

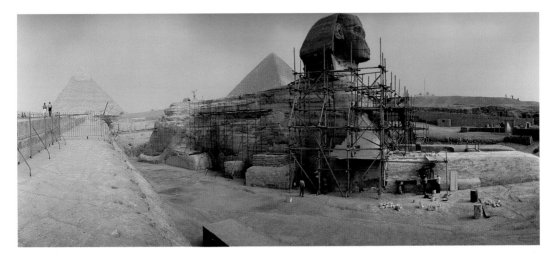

∧ The Great Sphinx has guarded the pyramids at Giza for thousands of years.

for their king. With great pride, the Egyptians created what was meant to be their king's home after death. Close to the Nile they built a valley temple that served as the entrance to the entire pyramid complex. Near the pyramid they constructed a mortuary temple where priests could perform daily rituals for their king. And connecting the two they built a long ramp—a causeway—a corridor leading from the entrance to the king's eternal palace. Behind it all, the pyramid soared skyward.

And who was all this for? The first generation of pyramid builders at Giza worked for Khufu who became king about 2551 B.C. The second generation worked for Khufu's son, Khafre. And the third for Khufu's grandson, Menkaure.

During those three generations, the Giza plateau was noisy and smoky, hustling and bustling. You wouldn't have been able to escape the thwack, thwack, thwack of thousands of hammers pounding copper chisels into rock. In the nearby horseshoe-shaped quarry, workmen carved blocks out of the limestone pit. They hammered chisels down four sides, and then forced wedges underneath to pop the block out. Once the workers had hauled the blocks from the quarry, stonemasons trimmed them, checking

< The view from the top of the Great Pyramid at Giza. At the time it was built, the plain below would have been home to thousands of workers.

∨ A worker brushes dust away from an inscription in a tomb found near Giza.

and rechecking the fit with the stones that were to be placed around them on the pyramid. The quarry rang with the sound of hundreds of stoneworkers hammering.

Noise was everywhere. Workmen grunted when they lifted stone blocks onto wooden sleds and shouted encouragement to their teammates. Ropes creaked under the strain. Water sloshed when full jars were dumped onto ramps to keep the tracks slick for sliding loaded sleds. And everywhere there was the chip-chip-chip of chisels. While the stonemasons worked outside, hundreds of artisans inscribed pictures and hieroglyphs on temple walls, causeways, courtyards, and columns.

∧ **This narrow passageway at the heart of the Great Pyramid is known as the Grand Gallery.**

A baker's tomb

Today the tombs and graves of the ordinary people who worked in the pyramid builders' city fascinate archaeologists almost as much as those of the pharaohs themselves. Near the pyramids, Hawass supervises the excavation of a baker's tomb. His name was Nefertheith. On the west wall of his tomb are three false doors for Nefertheith and his wives' spirits to pass through. Carved into the bottom of one door is a scene of people grinding grain and baking bread.

Another tomb Hawass is working on belongs to a teacher named Petety. Petety was Inspector of the Small Ones. Inscribed on a slab in his tomb is the curse, "Listen all of you! ... Anyone who does anything bad to my tomb, then the crocodile, the hippopotamus, and the lion will eat him."

Each year Hawass closes one pyramid for restoration work. The breath of visitors passing through Khufu's pyramid has added so much moisture to the air that there are places on the walls where salt has built up to three-quarters of an inch thick. The restoration team cleans away the salt. They update lighting, ventilation and security systems, repair cracks, and clean off graffiti.

The pyramids of Khufu and his descendants have filled people with wonder for 4,500 years. Thanks to the hard work and expertise of people like Dr. Hawass, it looks like they will continue to do so for thousands of years in the future.

Meet an Archaeologist

The head of the Supreme Council of Antiquities, Dr. Zahi Hawass is one of the best-known Egyptologists in the world. Here he answers some questions about the issues facing archaeologists today.

▣ Which mystery about ancient Egypt would you like to see solved?

▣ The first is solved already! Last year, we did a CT-scan of King Tut and found that he was not murdered, at least not by a blow on the back of the head. We also found out that he was well fed, and his mummy didn't show evidence of any childhood diseases. The other thing that I want to find out is what is behind the doors that I found inside the Great Pyramid. This is the real mystery to me.

▣ Which treasure would you like to see returned to Egypt?

▣ Over the last two years, I returned over 3,000 artifacts stolen from all over the world. But I would like to see the Rosetta Stone, the bust of Nefertiti, the Zodiac of Denderah, the statue of Hemuinu, architect of the Great Pyramid, and the bust of Ankhhaf, architect of the Second Pyramid, brought back to Egypt, at least for a visit. Right now, I would like the mask of Kanefernefer, which was stolen, to come back from the St. Louis Art Museum.

▣ Which past archaeological blunder would you like to see undone?

▣ There are many things done by archeologists in the past that I do not like. For example, the head of the Great Sphinx was restored with cement. I would like to correct this. Also, many excavations at Giza and Saqqara were not done scientifically. But the good thing is that I have re-excavated these sites and discovered things the earlier archaeologists missed.

▣ An archaeologist at KV-63 said that, to experts, coffins are as easy to date as cars are to Americans. Just as Americans can tell a 1920 Ford Model T from a 2006 Ford Mustang, you can distinguish an 18th Dynasty coffin from a 19th Dynasty model. What are some of the details of the KV-63 coffins that indicate that they came from the 18th Dynasty?

If you look at the face of the first coffin found in KV-63, you can see that the round cheeks, full lips, and nose are a lot like Tutankhamun's, and the wigs are like Yuya's and Tjuya's (probably Tutankhamun's great-grandparents).

You oversee an extraordinary number of exciting projects. Which project is the first one you think about when you wake up in the morning?
When I wake up in the morning, I think right away about revealing the secrets behind the doors in the Great Pyramid. We have looked behind one with a robot, and there is another slab blocking the way. Right now, I am deciding which team of robot experts to choose to look behind this block. And I have to think about how to protect the pyramid.

And are there any that keep you awake at night worrying?
I worry a lot about stolen artifacts. Antiquities thieves steal from all of us, and they are still taking our heritage. I wish that all the museums in the world would give back things that are stolen, and that no one would buy stolen artifacts. Then the thieves would have to stop.

There is a lot of controversy over DNA testing on mummies. What are your feelings on the subject?
We have to understand that getting accurate results from ancient DNA is very difficult, because it breaks down over time and it is hard to get a big enough sample. Also, it is easy to get a contaminated sample. But we are setting up a new lab dedicated to ancient DNA here in Egypt, different from a lab for modern DNA.

Egyptologist Zahi Hawass stands by the restored sarcophagus of the pharaoh Ramses VI.

A New Discovery

What else is hidden in the Valley of the Kings?

Would you be able to keep a secret for a whole year? A really, really big secret? That's what archaeologist Dr. Otto Schaden and his team had to do. They'd been digging in the Valley of the Kings at the request of Egypt's Supreme Council of Antiquities (SCA). The archaeologists were picking through 3,000-year-old workmen's huts, when suddenly they found what looked like the entrance to a tomb!

< The Valley of the Kings is home to the tombs of many New Kingdom pharaohs. Are there more discoveries to be made there?

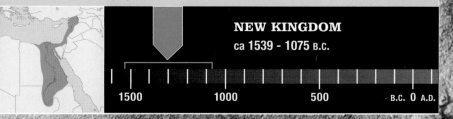

NEW KINGDOM
ca 1539 - 1075 B.C.

1500   1000   500   B.C. 0 A.D.

It was March 2005 and the digging season was almost over. Soaring temperatures baked the rock valley, turning it into an oven. The heat forced the team to take breaks more and more often to guzzle water and slather on sunscreen. Dr. Schaden had finished mapping the huts and would soon start refilling the pit. He said, "Suddenly we were coming across white chips. My workman couldn't understand why I was so excited." Afraid that it would turn out to be nothing, Dr Schaden tried to stay calm. But when his team cleared away more dust and rubble the outline of a shaft appeared.

Archaeologists believed that all the tombs in the Valley of the Kings had been uncovered. It had been more than 80 years since the last tomb— King Tut's—had been found. So imagine how difficult it was for Dr. Schaden and his colleagues to cover everything up, and wait until the next digging season to find out exactly what the team had discovered. Dr. Schaden must have lain awake many nights that year, tossing and turning and wondering. Was it a tomb? If so, had it been robbed, and was it now empty? Or would he find it undisturbed? What waited for him at the bottom of that shaft?

Opening the tomb

The following January Dr. Schaden's team returned to the Valley of the Kings and began clearing the elevator-like shaft of limestone chips and rocks. They'd dug more than 14 feet (4 m) down when they uncovered an entrance made of stone blocks. What lay behind that door? Would it be an empty room? Some forgotten, unused chamber? The archaeologists gently pulled away rubble. A rush of hot myrrh-scented air huffed into their faces. Then, after almost an entire year, Dr. Schaden took his first look into the room. The chamber was not empty. In fact, it was jam-packed with storage jars and coffins. It was time to tell the whole world about the discovery.

◁ The entrance to KV-63, partially blocked with stones. It lay at the foot of a shaft that had remained hidden for centuries.

< This mask decorates one of the coffins found at KV-63. Some historians believe that the yellow skin indicates that the coffin was made for a woman.

∨ A large number of ceramic storage jars were found inside KV-63. Among other things, they contained seeds, fragments of papyrus, and pieces of pottery.

The unveiling

In February 2006 Dr. Zahi Hawass, the head of the SCA, officially unveiled the tomb, which was now called KV-63 as it was the 63rd tomb to be found in the Valley of the Kings. But was it really a tomb? To properly study the chamber's contents and answer that question, everything had to be removed from the cramped quarters. The jars could be moved with care, but some of the coffins were far too fragile. Termites had spent 3,000 years munching on the wood until it was paper thin. The coffins were just a jumble of splinters

held together by the resin the ancient Egyptians had poured over the top. The slightest touch could reduce them to dust.

Nadia Lokma, the chief curator of the Egyptian Museum in Cairo

< Dr. Otto Schaden holds a miniature gold coffin that was found at KV-63.

and an expert in wood conservation, was called in to help. Carefully, she stuffed the damaged coffin lids with cotton soaked in fluids that bound the wood fragments together and hardened them into a shell. Then she covered the still delicate wood with tissue paper and painted it with reinforcing fluids.

As the days wore on, the temperatures rose to a stifling 130°F (54°C). Even the wind brought no relief. But once the tomb had been opened they could not stop until it was emptied. With the tomb unsealed, the contents were exposed to changing air and were extremely vulnerable. Even though the digging season was long over, the team continued a job that could not be rushed.

Time after time the hardships were forgotten because of the fantastic nature of the discoveries. One coffin contained a set of pillows, an extreme rarity. The finely woven fabric was marked with hieroglyphs that said "life, health, and wealth." And buried in the pillows was a spectacular, baby-sized gold coffinette. In the last sarcophagus opened, the team found a collar of flowers. Lokma said, "It's very rare— there's nothing like it in any museum. We've seen things like it in drawings, but we've never seen this before in real life. It's magnificent."

▽ **This is one of seven coffins found at KV-63. Unlike some, it was in a very good condition when it was discovered.**

The work continues

KV-63 is empty now. The small room at the bottom of the shaft that for thousands of years had been crammed full of pots and coffins is bare. Some articles have been moved to a nearby tomb, KV-10, for conservation and further study. Samples from the jars, coffin fragments, and other pieces were taken to Cairo where experts will examine them.

The work on KV-63 has only just begun. There are decades of study ahead. And some important questions to be answered. Was KV-63 really a tomb? No

mummies were found there, just empty coffins. Archaeologists now believe that the chamber was actually an embalmer's storeroom. But questions still remain. Who were the coffins made for? And when will the next new discovery be made?

> **A storage jar is lifted from KV-63 so that it can be taken away and examined.**

CHAPTER 7

Saving the Temples

How do we protect the wonders of the past?

The early 21st century is proving to be an exciting time for Egyptologists. The first years of the century saw a number of fascinating finds. As well as KV-63, archaeologists also discovered an elaborately decorated mummy at Saqqara and a statue of the pharaoh Neferhotep I at Luxor. And in 2001 a team of French archaeologists found the remains of a lion that had been ritually buried.

New technology is helping archaeologists to explore areas that their predecessors could only have dreamed of. In 2002 a team of scientists sent

< The statue of Ramses II stands in its former home in Cairo. It has now been removed to protect it from traffic fumes and other forms of pollution.

∧ American scientists test the Pyramid Rover, which was later sent into the heart of the Great Pyramid.

a miniature robot, nicknamed the Pyramid Rover, to explore a shaft in the Great Pyramid at Giza. The robot drilled a hole in a limestone door blocking the shaft, allowing human eyes to see beyond it for the first time in thousands of years. And what did they see? Another door! One mystery had been solved just for a new one to be created.

But discovering new tombs isn't the only thing on the minds of Egyptologists. As well as finding new treasures, they have to worry about protecting the great monuments of the past.

Sometimes the solution can seem relatively easy. One famous monument that was threatened by pollution was the giant statue of Ramses II that

stood in Ramses Square in Cairo between 1955 and 2006. The 3,200-year-old figure was endangered by the city's traffic fumes and vibrations from its subway system, so a decision was made to transport it to a safer place. In August 2006, the statue was put on the back of a truck and taken to a new location near the great pyramids where it will one day be housed in a new museum.

Some things are harder to protect, however. Many of ancient Egypt's greatest monuments are threatened with pollution, and you can't put the pyramids or the Sphinx on the back of a truck and move them to safety! How to save these great relics of the past is a huge challenge for Egyptologists.

Moving the Temple

The idea of moving a monument in its entirety to protect it from the environment may seem far-fetched, but it has happened before.

One of Egypt's most spectacular ancient sites is the temple complex at Abu Simbel, which was carved out of the mountainside during the reign of Ramses II in the 13th century B.C. The main temple features four giant statues of the pharaoh.

The temples were situated at Lake Nasser and by the the 1960s they were being threatened by rising water levels caused by the building of the Aswan Dam. In an incredibly complex operation, the temples were completely dismantled and reassembled 195 feet (59m) further up the cliff. The operation lasted from 1964 until 1966. The temple complex is one of Egypt's most popular tourist attractions.

∧ The head of one of the four statues of Ramses II at Abu Simbel is moved as part of the operation to save the temple.

> The main temple at Abu Simbel as it appears today, after its successful relocation

The Years Ahead

Exhaust fumes from cars. Moisture from the breath of tourists. Leaking sewage systems. There are all sorts of dangers facing Egypt's relics of the past. One that is causing particular concern is the rising water table (the upper level of water in the ground). The water brings salt with it, and salt destroys limestone. If nothing is done, many of ancient Egypt's great temples will be turned into dust.

But something is being done. Two areas under threat are the temple complexes of Karnak and Luxor, which stand near one another on the site of the ancient city of Thebes. In recent years the water level has risen up to five feet (1.5 m) threatening the foundations of the temples.

In response, a complicated system of pumps and drainage trenches is being put in place to direct water away from the immediate area. If the scheme is successful, Karnak and Luxor will be saved. But the fight to preserve Egypt's heritage will go on.

▽ The ruins of the temple complex at Karnak have been under threat from a rise in the water table.

Glossary

afterlife – an existence after death

artifact – any object changed by human activity

cemetery – a place where a number of dead bodies are buried

circa – about; used to indicate a date that is approximate and abbreviated as ca

conservator – a scientist who works to protect ancient objects or buildings from further damage

corps – a body of soldiers

CT scan – a 3-D image made by x-ray cameras and computers

curator – a person who organizes and looks after a collection of objects or pictures

diplomatic language – the language that different governments use to communicate with one another

draftsman – a person who draws plans for creating buildings or other objects

Egyptologist – an expert who studies aspects of ancient Egypt

embalmer – a person who treats a dead body with chemicals to prepare it for burial

excavation – an archaeological dig

granite – a very hard type of rock

hieroglyphics – a system of writing with pictures developed by the Egyptians

mortuary temples – temples where the bodies of the dead were stored before burial

mummy – an embalmed and preserved dead body

pharaoh – a ruler of ancient Egypt

pollution – exhaust fumes, smoke, and other substances that make the air or water dirty

pyramid – a burial monument with a square base and four sides that rise to a point

sarcophagus – a stone coffin

sphinx – a monument with the head of a man but the body of a lion

stonemason – a craftsperson who prepares blocks of stone used in making buildings

tomb – a place where a dead body is kept

underworld – the place where the dead live in the afterlife

Bibliography

Books

Baines, John, and Jaromir Malek. *Atlas of Ancient Egypt*. New York: Facts On File, Inc., 2002.

Egypt: Land of the Pharaohs (Lost Civilizations). Alexandria, Va.: Time-Life Books, 1992.

Hawass, Zahi. *The Golden King: The World of Tutankhamun*. Washington, D.C.: National Geographic, 2004.

Hawass, Zahi. *Mountains of the Pharaohs: The Untold Story of the Pyramid Builders*. New York: Doubleday, 2006.

Articles

Hawass, Zahi. "Egypt's Forgotten Treasures." NATIONAL GEOGRAPHIC (January 2003): 74–87

Weeks, Kent R. "Valley of the Kings." NATIONAL GEOGRAPHIC (September 1998): 2–33

Williams, A. R. "Death on the Nile." NATIONAL GEOGRAPHIC (October 2002): 2–25

Zivie, Alain. "Mystery of the Sun God's Servant." NATIONAL GEOGRAPHIC (November 2003): 52–59

Further Reading

Ancient Egypt (Eyewitness Books). New York: Dorling Kindersley, 2004.

Langley, Andrew. *Ancient Egypt* (History in Art). Chicago: Raintree, 2005.

Mummy (Eyewitness Books). New York: Dorling Kindersley, 2004.

Pyramid (Eyewitness Books). New York: Dorling Kindersley, 2004.

Ross, Stewart. *Ancient Egypt* (Ancient Civilizations). Milwaukee, Wis: Gareth Stevens Publishing, 2005.

Web Sites

British Museum Ancient Egypt site
http://www.ancientegypt.co.uk/menu.html

History for Kids Ancient Egypt index
http://www.historyforkids.org/learn/egypt/index.htm

National Geographic: Explore the Pyramids
http://www.nationalgeographic.com/pyramids

UNESCO World Heritage List for Egypt
http://whc.unesco.org/en/statesparties/eg

Index

Boldface indicates illustrations.

< This statue of
the Egyptian king
Menkaure was made
in around 2500 B.C.
He is flanked by
two goddesses.

About the Author

JILL RUBALCABA began her career as a college and high school mathematics teacher, all the while continuing to go to school to study more math, writing, and business. She lives in Kennebunk, Maine, with her family and their cat, Scribbles. Ms. Rubalcaba is grateful to her children, Kelly and Dan, for showing her the joys of writing for children. She is the author of several children's books on ancient Egypt—*The Ancient Egyptian World*, *The Wadjet Eye,* and *A Place in the Sun*. This is her first book for National Geographic.

About the Consultant

JANICE KAMRIN received her Ph.D. in Egyptian Archaeology from the University of Pennsylvania. She has taught at a number of universities, including the American University in Cairo, and given many lectures to general audiences on ancient Egypt. She currently works with Dr. Zahi Hawass, Secretary General of the Supreme Council of Antiquities of Egypt, on many of his popular publications, and serves as a consultant to the SCA and the Egyptian Museum, Cairo. Her most recent publication is *Hieroglyphs for Children*, available in both English and Arabic.

Sources for Quotations

Page 18: Reeves, Nicholas. *Ancient Egypt: The Great Discoveries*. New York: Thames & Hudson, 2000.
Page 22: Budge, E. A. Wallis. *By Nile and Tigris*. London: J. Murray, 1920.
Page 28: Chamberlain, Ted. "King Tut Mummy Scanned—Could Solve Murder Mystery." *National Geographic News* (January 6, 2005).
Page 37: McDowell, A. G. *Village Life in Ancient Egypt: Laundry Lists and Love Songs*. New York: Oxford University Press, 1999.

Page 39: Editors of Time-Life Books. *What Life Was Like on the Banks of the Nile*. Alexandria, Va.: Time-Life Books, 1996.
Page 45: Hawass, Zahi. *Secrets from the Sand: My Search for Egypt's Past*. New York: Harry N. Abrams, 2003.
Page 50: Akshar, Jane. "The Discovery in West Thebes." www.touregypt.net.
Page 52: Montesquiou, Alfred de. "New Tomb in Egypt Reveals Flowers not Mummies." *Mail & Guardian Online* (June 29, 2006).

One of the world's largest nonprofit
scientific and educational organizations, the
National Geographic Society was founded in
1888 "for the increase and diffusion of
geographic knowledge." Fulfilling this
mission, the Society educates and inspires millions
every day through its magazines, books, television
programs, videos, maps and atlases, research grants,
the National Geographic Bee, teacher workshops, and
innovative classroom materials. The Society is
supported through membership dues, charitable gifts,
and income from the sale of its educational products.
This support is vital to National Geographic's mission
to increase global understanding and promote
conservation of our planet through exploration,
research, and education.

For more information, please call 1-800-NGS-LINE
(647-5463) or write to the following address:

National Geographic Society
1145 17th Street N.W.
Washington, D.C. 20036-4688
U.S.A.

Visit the Society's Web site:
www.nationalgeographic.com

Library of Congress Cataloging-in-Publication Data
available upon request
Hardcover ISBN-10: 0-7922-7784-8
        ISBN-13: 978-0-7922-7784-2
Library Edition ISBN-10: 0-7922-7857-7
        ISBN-13: 978-0-7922-7857-3

Printed in Mexico

Series design by Jim Hiscott
The body text is set in Century Schoolbook
The display text is set in Helvetica Neue, Clarendon

National Geographic Society

John M. Fahey, Jr., *President and Chief Executive
Officer;* Gilbert M. Grosvenor, *Chairman of the Board;*
Nina D. Hoffman, *Executive Vice President, President of
Books Publishing Group*

Staff for This Book

Nancy Laties Feresten, *Vice President, Editor-in-Chief
of Children's Books*
Virginia Ann Koeth, *Project Editor*
Bea Jackson, *Director of Design and Illustration*
David Seager, *Art Director*
Lori Epstein, Greta Arnold, National Geographic Image
Sales, *Illustrations Editors*
Jean Cantu, *Illustrations Specialist*

Carl Mehler, *Director of Maps*
Priyanka Lamichhane, *Assistant Editor*
R. Gary Colbert, *Production Director*
Lewis R. Bassford, *Production Manager*
Vincent P. Ryan, Maryclare Tracy, *Manufacturing
Managers*

For the Brown Reference Group, plc

Tim Cooke, *Managing Editor*
Alan Gooch, *Book Designer*
Becky Cox, *Picture Researcher*

Photo Credits

Front cover: ©Claudius/Zefa/Corbis
Spine: © Carolyn Brown/ Getty Images
Back cover: Background image: gds/sefa/Corbis;
Figure: © British Museum, London, Great
Britain/Werner Forman/ Art Resource, NY
Icon: © Connors Bros./Shutterstock

All images, except as noted below are by Kenneth
Garrett/National Geographic Image Collection.
NGIC = National Geographic Image Collection
1, © British Museum, London, Great Britain; 2-3, ©
Jose Fuste Raga/Corbis; 4, © Dagli Orti/The Art
Archive; 6, © Carolyn Brown/Getty Images; 8, ©
Gustavo Camps; 10, © Roger Woods/Corbis; 11, ©
Bettmann/Corbis; 14, © Christies Images/Corbis; 15
bottom, © Erich Lessing/AKG Images; 16, © Egyptian
Museum/Werner Forman Archive; 17 top, © Erick
Lessing/AKG Images; 17 bottom, © Herve
Champollion/AKG Images; 18, © Hulton Deutsch
Collection/Corbis; 22, © Musée du Lourve, Paris/Dagli
Orti/The Art Archive; 23, © François Guenet/AKG
Images; 25 bottom, © Emory Kristof/National
Geographic Image Collection; 28, © Egyptian
Museum/AKG Images; 30 left, © Hulton Deutsch
Collection/Corbis; 30 right, © Stapleton
Collection/Corbis; 34 top, © Musée du Louvre,
Paris/Dagli Orti/The Art Archive; 34 bottom, © E.
Strohal/Werner Forman Archive; 36-37, © C. F. Payne
/NGIC; 38 bottom, © Erick Lessing/AKG Images; 40-41,
© O. Louis Mazzatenta/NGIC; 42, © William H.
Bond/NGIC; 43 top, © Herve Champollion/AKG
Images; 43 bottom, © James L. Stanfield; 44 bottom, ©
Reuters/Corbis; 46, © Tannen Maury/EPA/Corbis; 47, ©
Aladin Abdel Naby/Reuters/Corbis; 48-49, © K. M.
Westermann/Corbis; 50, © Heather Alexander/www.KV-
63.com; 51 top, © Roxanne Wilson/www.KV-63.com; 51
bottom, © Roxanne Wilson/www.KV-63.com; 52, © Elise
Van Rooij/www.KV-63.com; 53 top © Heather
Alexander/www.KV-63.com; 53 bottom, © Roxanne
Wilson/www.KV-63.com; 54-55, © Herve
Champollion/AKG Images; 56, © Reuters/Corbis; 57
top, © Robert Caputo/NGIC; 57 bottom, © George
Gerster/NGIC; 58, © Wildcountry/Corbis; 63, ©
Egyptian Museum, Cairo/Werner Forman Archive.

Front cover: The gold funerary mask of the
pharaoh Tutankhamun, now housed in the Egyptian
Museum, Cairo
Page 1 and back cover: A small painted vase in the
form of a fish, found at Amarna
Pages 2–3: Tourists wander among the pillars of the
Hypostyle Hall at Karnak.